W9-CCQ-115

Table of Contents

Introduction

My determined purpose is that I may know Him, that I may progressively become more deeply and intimately acquainted with Him, perceiving and recognizing and understanding the wonders of His person.
Philippians 3:10 (Amplified Bible)

One of the greatest yearnings of the human heart is to know there is a purpose to life. To know there is a reason we are here on this earth. And in this one verse Paul sets out the true purpose to life—the one which can only bring the fulfillment our hearts yearn for.

In the next few pages I want to help you understand the power of Paul's words and the wonder and beauty they can bring to your life.

These words first struck me one

Discovering

God's

Purpose

for Your Life

Living Proof

with Beth Moore

Discovering God's Purpose for Your Life

Published by
DUNHAM BOOKS
15455 Dallas Parkway, Sixth Floor, Addison, Texas 75001

©2004 by Beth Moore
and Living Proof Ministries®
Published 2005

Third Printing

ISBN: 0-9787638-0-7

Unless otherwise noted, all scripture quotations
are taken from the
NEW INTERNATIONAL VERSION

Printed in the United States of America

For information:
Living Proof Ministries
PO Box 840849
Houston TX   77084
lproof@lproof.org

morning as I was spending time with God, reading His Word. While Philippians 3:10 has been one of my all-time favorite verses, I had never quite seen it as God wanted me to until I read it in the Amplified Bible.

This verse kept rolling over and over in my mind. I knew God was trying to speak to me—to show me the power of what He had inspired Paul to write. Then it struck me. Notice Paul's words. *Perceiving, recognizing and understanding.* Not just what He can do, although that is critical. Not just what He can give me, although He is the giver of all good gifts. But Paul said, I want to perceive, I want to recognize, I want to understand the wonders of His own personhood more strongly and more clearly.

In the next few pages, I want to take this verse apart for you. As I do, my hope for you is that God will reveal to you the power of these words—and that you would experience, as I have, the radical transformation that can occur when you embrace and apply this truth.

Chapter One

My Determined Purpose...

These first three words are incredibly powerful words. It is not an accident Paul uses the word *"my"* to begin this verse. It is so easy for us to focus on the lives of others. We are great at seeing in them the need for change. The need to get their act together. But, beloved, when we're into so many other people's business, we can't attend to our own business with God.

I've a mark on me that God has used to clearly reveal the reality of this truth. Recently I was on a walk with my dogs, and we came around a corner and five feet from us was a rabbit. Immediately my bird dog was off that leash and running. I tried to grab the rope of the leash and when I did it went across my palm, burning me right across the hand. Today I bear the mark of trying to hang on to something that didn't want me hanging on to it!

As I have looked at that scar I've come to realize I bear the marks of trying to hang on to people and things too tightly. I have especially tried to hang on to my children too tightly and I'm sure I have some of my husband's skin under my fingernails!

I am challenging you to open your mind and heart so God can do something huge in your life.

We all have those people we love so much, and we just believe they need fixin', and they need bossin', and they need manipulatin', and they need controllin'! And we're so busy focusing on them that we haven't had a fresh work of God in months—and maybe years—in our own lives because we're waiting for Him to have a fresh work in somebody else's life.

You cannot determine anybody else's purpose for them. But I'll tell you what you can do. You can determine God's purpose for your life. I am challenging you to open your mind and heart so God can do something huge in your life. Nobody can do this for you, but you can make up your mind right now to pursue God's purpose for your life.

The word right after "my" is

The actual spoken word is indeed powerful when we make a profession, a confession of our faith.

"determined." This is a fascinating word. I was personally blown away when I learned the definition of the word "determination." According to the dictionary I used, it says determination is "the act of making or arriving at a decision; the quality of being resolute or firm in purpose; the act of settling a dispute…."

As I thought about that I realized this is

the kind of determination God calls us to. So often one of the greatest things that keeps you and me from realizing God's purpose in our life is the dispute within us. It is a war within us, a fight within us, within our inner man. The things of the soul are at war with the things of the Spirit.

Now, right now, you can win that dispute. How? By choosing to make the focus of your life knowing Him. By making that the purpose of your life. If you were to make that decision right now, I guarantee you, it would be completely life altering.

In fact, that is the only way you will settle the dispute in your heart. As I read on, the definition of "determination" said, "The act of settling a dispute or other question, by an authoritative decision or pronouncement."

I love that. Why? Because we are told in Scripture we are to renounce sin. While we want the thoughts of Christ to literally dwell in our minds, and we know our thoughts are absolutely critical (for "as a man thinketh, so is he"), yet there is even more power when we speak—verbally renounce—our sin. The actual spoken word is indeed powerful when we make a profession, a confession of our faith.

I believe this is what Paul, prompted by the Holy Spirit, is saying to you and me in this passage. We must make a pronouncement of a made-up mind. A pronouncement of a determination to know Him.

Now I want to show you something really incredible. I am sure you are familiar with the Old Testament word "covenant." In Genesis chapter 15, God made a covenant with Abram (interestingly, in the Hebrew it literally says that God "cut a covenant" with Abram). And then we're told in the New Testament we are under the "New Covenant." In Hebrew "covenant" is the word "berett." If you looked that word up in your Hebrew dictionary, you would find the word not only means "covenant," but it also means "determination."

I believe God is trying to help you and me understand His determination in His pursuit of us. God has made a new covenant—a new determination—with you and me through Jesus Christ. And He will never let up in that determination. He keeps after us, and keeps after us, and will never tire in that pursuit. And what I want you to understand is that when God cut His covenant with us through Jesus Christ, He was determined in His pursuit of us.

He is determined to pursue you because He knows the greatest joy in your life will come from His plan for you.

I want you to know that, because I want you to understand just how significant and precious you are to God. He's got a made-up mind where you're concerned. He knows how He wants your life to pan out. Our God knows the end from the beginning. And He is determined to pursue you because He knows the greatest joy in your life will come from His plan for you.

So here's what I want you to understand. If you will receive the fact that God is determined where you are concerned, and you will get determined where He is concerned, your life will be radically transformed. You will experience huge, miraculous, unexplainable things.

When you accept the fact that God is determined about you, and you add to it your

We can live with all manner of tribulation more easily than we can live with purposelessness.

determination about Him, I am telling you, there'll be no stopping you from fulfilling the absolutely God-ordained destiny He has for you. So let me ask you, are you determined?

"My determined purpose." Now I love this third word, "purpose." And I want you

to think about it just a second. As I have
thought about this, here is what I have come
to realize. I am quite sure we can live with
pain, and we can live with suffering, and we
can live with all manner of tribulation more
easily than we can live with purposelessness.
We can get through almost anything if we
know there is purpose.

But I'm telling you, there is an emptiness
in your life even if you're in Christ, if you
have not discovered that you have purpose
in Him. And how great that emptiness if
you have not figured out what on earth His
purpose is for you.

This sense of purpose, I believe, is not
a spiritual state; it's an emotional and mental
state in which we just can't seem to put life
together without a sense of purpose. Why?
Because you and I were created to be a people
who seek purpose.

God did not set Adam in the garden to
cultivate it after the fall, but rather He set him
in it before the fall. Why? Because He knew

man was created with the need to contribute and to feel a genuine sense of purpose. It gives life meaning every single moment if we know we have a purpose.

So let me ask you, do you know what your purpose is? God knows what it is, and if you determine the same purpose in your life that God has determined for you, I am telling you that's when your life will explode with true fulfillment. But you will not experience that fulfillment until then. Until then, you will always have that seeking, that sense of dissatisfaction, that sense of not being able to fully grasp a fulfilled and happy life.

In his wonderful book, *The Purpose Driven Life*, Rick Warren writes these words —I want you to read these carefully:

There is nothing quite as potent as a focused life. One lived on purpose.

Do you understand what he is saying? Focus. Focus. He goes on to say:

You become effective by becoming selective.

You and I become effective by becoming selective. One reason we lack effectiveness in the sphere of influence that we have is because our minds (Moms?!?) are just wigged out from one extreme to the other. We live two miles wide and a half an inch deep. We are totally caught up in a thousand different things, and not doing any of them well.

I remember when my daughter Melissa was a child. She had enough energy to climb a 20 foot brick wall. This is a child who rode a two-wheeler, no training wheels, a couple of days before her third birthday. This was my wild child.

You and I become effective by becoming selective.

And then about the fourth grade, after this child had driven us crazy and just pitched us every which way, somebody put a basketball in her hands. The first time she shot the ball it was nothin' but net. It was at that point that I stood back and thought, "Mm, mm, mm. That's what it's gonna be." Now, I really didn't care much about basketball— oh, I learned to care about it. In fact, I was the most obnoxious person in the stands by the time she was a junior—but all of a sudden, Melissa had a focus to her life.

Now let me ask you, wouldn't it be a relief to you if you were all about one thing? But I have to tell you, if you are to live out God's purpose for your life, you must come to a place where you determine a focus to your life. God has designed an excellence, a single purpose for you and me.

If you are to live out God's purpose for your life, you must come to a place where you determine a focus to your life.

I have thought about this so many times because I have so often lived with a divided heart. But, let me tell you, divided loyalties can be the death of us.

Oh, sure, we will say, "God, You are the most important thing." And then we kind of line everything up behind that. But what He's trying to get through to us is this: He is not the most important thing, He is the ONLY thing. He is it. He is your life—not just a part of it, or even the most important thing in your life. He is everything.

Paul says it this way in Colossians 3:4,

When Christ, who is your life, appears...

WOW! Those are powerful words. Paul says, He is your life. And when your life becomes totally focused on Him—when everything becomes that one thing, that one stream, and that focus on Him begins to impact how you do everything, and everything you go through is about that one thing—let me tell you something, your life will be radically transformed.

Selective becomes effective.

I want you to carefully read these next words by George Bernard Shaw. When I read them they stunned me. They made me sit back and really think.

> *This is the true joy in life,*
> *the being used for a purpose*
> *recognized by yourself as a mighty*
> *one... the being a force of Nature*
> *instead of a feverish, selfish little*
> *clod of ailments and grievances*
> *complaining that the world will*
> *not devote itself to making you*
> *happy.* (Man and Superman, Epistle
> Dedicatory)

Whoa! Pouring ourselves out for one purpose. That is what must consume you and me instead of being a selfish, feverish little clod that grieves and despairs because the world will not determine to make us happy.

Purpose. Determination. A single-minded focus in all of life. Does that apply to your life? Or are you wandering through your life without any purpose?

I heard somebody say the other day, "I'm still trying to figure out what I want to be when I grow up." And you know what? We laugh about that—while we

color our roots! But we are grown up!
Perhaps not in the things of the faith, but
we are grown-ups. And it's time to determine
what our purpose is.

I want to know Christ. What about you?
Paul says, "I want to know Christ!"

Chapter Two

Is that I may know Him...

The next phrase of Phillipians 3:10 tells us our one purpose. First, I want you to look at that word "know." "My determined purpose is that I may know...." I want you to carefully reflect on that word because it is just so critical.

It tells us so clearly that this is the purpose—to know.

Isaiah 43:10 says, *"You are my witnesses," declares the LORD, "and my servant whom I have chosen, so that you may know and believe me and understand that I am he."* Jeremiah 9:24 says, *"let him who boasts boast about this: that he understands and knows me."*

Our determined purpose is to know God.

I can remember being told early on by an editor, "Now, Beth, when you're writing, keep to your subject matter." I'm one of those who would chase every rabbit you can imagine. He said, "Ask yourself in every paragraph, ask yourself on every page, 'Is it true to the one primary thing you are trying to say?'" Now, I not only apply this to my writing, I have started adopting this rule even in speaking.

Your book— your life— is named *Knowing Christ,* and it is by you.

Take a moment to think about your own book—your life. On the front of your book is a title. And that title should be the same one for every single one of us: *Knowing Christ.* Then under the title is a line that says, "by," and that's where you would put your name.

You can pick out your own colors for your cover, you can decorate it any way you want, any thought you want. But here is

what I want you to get in head: Your book—
your life—is named *Knowing Christ,* and it
is by you.

Every single chapter is focused on
that one thing. Now I don't know about you,
but I find that my seasons—the chapters in
my life—will sometimes last three to four
years. And it seems that very often when I'm
going through something, when I go through
a particular season, it's all about one
prevailing thing.

For example, as I write this, the one
chapter I'm living in right now is "Knowing
Christ in the Whirlwind." I feel like I'm just
in a whirlwind. I couldn't tell you if it was
negative or positive. I'm just trying to keep
the dust of the earth from getting in my eyes!

And the last chapter I was living was
"Knowing Christ in the Rubble." I remember
going through a season of time of so much
change and so much loss that it was like
I'd been standing on a nice spacious piece
of concrete and God just came in with a

jackhammer and unearthed everything around me except that size 7 right under my feet. Perhaps you know what I'm talking about!

What in the world do you do when He's turning up every bit of ground around you except what you're standing on? Child, you be still and know He is God. You be still, because there is no place for you to step!! Everything seems like an earthquake except where you're standing and that is a "Be still" moment.

What would your chapter right now be called? This is so important for you to get in your mind because this is what it's all about. In every single season of our lives, in every situation, in every circumstance, He is after you knowing Him. This is the most marvelous

In every single season of our lives, in every situation, in every circumstance, He is after you knowing Him.

purpose in the world. And catch this: there

is not one season in your life in which you cannot know Him. It does not exist. In every single season there is a fresh opportunity to know Christ. And that's what we're about.

Now you might be thinking, "But, Beth, the first commandment, the priority commandment, is that we should love Him." Let me tell you something—to know Him is to love Him. Or you might say, "But, Beth, we're supposed to serve Him." I promise

To know Christ, is to perceive what He is saying to us through His Word.

you, when you know Him, you will love Him, and no one will be able to stop you from serving Him. In fact, don't even talk to me about loving Him and knowing Him

if you are staying home and not pouring into the body of Christ and not reaching out to the lost. Why? Because, when you and I have witnessed Him, we will witness Him to others. Nobody has to tell us to do it. It is the most supernatural and natural occurrence we could possibly have in the faith. When we witness Him, we will witness Him to others.

To know Him. This word "know" is so powerful. Let me show you what some of the wonderful definitions are in the Greek language.

First, this word "know" in the Greek transliteration is "genasco." It generally means "acquired knowledge." And this knowledge is primarily acquired through perception. That understanding is very important to keep in mind. In fact, the word "genasco" to a very great extent means "to perceive." In other words, when we read God's Word, we cannot read it with the eyes of the natural man and even understand what God is trying to say. It is supernaturally perceived.

So to know Christ is to perceive what He is saying to us through His Word. Do you get that? You cannot know Christ until you perceive His truth through His word.

This is something I've wanted my daughters to understand. I have told them,

"Don't you even think about looking at that Book like just a normal book of 'how to's and 'what to's. You ask God to jump that Word off the page, to make that thing become 3-D. To have it just turn fluorescent for you."

And I challenge you to the same thing. I challenge you to pray the words of the 119th Psalm, *Show me the wonders of your Word.*

My prayer, my cry is, "Thrill me with Your Word. Delight me with Your Word. Make this my bread and my meat. Cause me to perceive You through what I read, through what I see, through what I experience. Disclose yourself to me. Give me perception."

I challenge you, make that your prayer, too!

As we consider this idea of knowing Christ, we need to understand what that means at even a deeper level. In Philippians 3:8 it says this: *What is more, I consider everything a loss compared to the surpassing greatness of knowing Christ Jesus my Lord.*

In this verse Paul uses the noun form of this same verb "to know." That word in the transliterated Greek is "nosis." Now this is the noun form of the word for "knowledge," and in some translations you will see this word in this passage translated as "the knowledge." But it is something more intentional than that. What this word means when it is distinguished from other similar words is this: it implies present and fragmentary knowledge.

It's very important that you get that. Present and fragmentary knowledge. A fragment of real knowledge. This is important because what Paul is implying here (that you and I cannot understand and distinguish in our English language) is this: "The little that I know, the fragments that I have, are worth the loss of everything I've had to give up to know it."

"Now we see but a poor reflection as in a mirror; then we shall see face to face."

Do you understand what he's saying? This little bit, this little fragment of Christ would be worth the loss of everything else that I identify myself by. These fragments of knowledge I've gained about Christ along the way are worth everything to me. Isn't that an amazing thing?

But the good stuff doesn't stop there. Let me show you another word which is found in I Corinthians chapter 13,

My determined purpose is to grab as many fragments of knowledge about Christ Jesus my Lord through this lifetime as is humanly possible.

When I was a child, I talked like a child, I thought like a child, I reasoned like a child. When I became a man, I put childish ways behind me. Now we see but a poor reflection as in a mirror; then we shall see face to face. Now I know in part; then I shall know fully, even as I am fully known.

Now I don't want you to miss the

importance of this passage, because it takes this word for knowledge that we've been looking at, this present and fragmentary knowledge, and suddenly it gives us the hope of "full and complete" knowledge.

Paul's point is that our goal in life is to pull together as many of these fragments of knowledge about who Christ is...what He does, what His ways are like...as possible. So as we go through life—through every single season—we need to see that every situation gives us opportunity to pull together another fragment, and another fragment, and another fragment, and another fragment. And what we're looking for while we're walking on this planet is to pull together enough of those fragments so we have a working knowledge of who our God is.

But then one day when we see Him face to face, we will have all these little fragments laying out in front of us that we will bring before Him like pieces before an altar, and in a millisecond it will be made one piece...

complete. And that is the goal.

My determined purpose is that I may know Him.

My determined purpose is to grab as many fragments of knowledge about Christ Jesus my Lord through this lifetime as is humanly possible. So that when I see Him face to face, He can take those fragments and make them complete. At that moment I will know Him, as I've been known.

In this life who we are is all about Who we know.

Chapter Three

That I may progressively become more deeply and intimately acquainted with Him...

Now how does this all go together? Read again Philippians 3:10.

My determined purpose is that I may know Him, that I may progressively become....

"Progressively" is the next word I want you to think about, because here's what happens. After we come to faith in Christ, we begin to move along in our spiritual walk, but at a certain point we just get to a place where our faith becomes business as usual. It's enjoyable, it's fulfilling to us in many ways.

But our knowledge of Him is about the same as it was a year ago. And about the same as five years ago.

We end up at that place where we couldn't really tell you the last time God just shook us up with a fresh knowledge of who He is according to His Word. In fact, we get into the trap where we just read the same things over and over so that we can reconfirm what we already believe. We march ourselves to a Christian bookstore, and we pass by everything that's not familiar to get to what is familiar. And so we just keep reaffirming the same old thing over and over again.

But what we need to do is let Him shake us up a little bit. We need to pray, "Lord, tell me something new about You." We need to progressively grow in our knowledge of Him. We need to be women and men who know our God progressively and more intimately.

So why don't we? Here is what I think hangs us up. We don't believe it's worth it. After all, why would we put all our life's energy and purpose into knowing one person? When it all comes down, isn't that really it? We think, "I'm going to be there for eternity, so can't we do that then? I have a lot to do here. Why in the world would I want to spend my life getting to know Him better?"

Let me tell you why. Because of the wonders of His person. Oh, please don't check out on me here. Giving your life to knowing Christ more intimately is worth

We need to pray, "Lord, tell me something new about You."

it because of the wonders of His person. Sadly, we don't believe this because we have compared and measured Christ according to a human standard.

How does that play out? Let me tell you. We meet someone really, really interesting and decide we want to get to know them. So after a few lunches and some time together we feel like we know them! We think, "I'm so relieved I don't have to go out with them for lunch for six months…I already know them!" Amen?

And we think God's like that.

Now, what we have to understand is God has built into us a desire for intimacy. The deep desire of the heart and soul for relationship. It's that yearning I have seen fulfilled in my daughters. It is the sweetest thing to watch.

My youngest one is head over heels in love with a young man who is six-and-a-half feet tall. And I have watched them—they

What we have to understand is God has built into us a desire for intimacy. cannot get enough of looking at each other. One night we were going out to dinner and I literally had to get between them

and say, "Hello? Do you remember me? My name is Mother. I birthed you in pain and travail! And I have a simple question for you—are you going with us to eat, or not?"

They are so cute!

I've asked her over and over again, "Tell me something new you're learning about him." See, they're in that stage where they want to have a date until midnight and then they want to talk on the phone until three in the morning. Why? Because they just can't get enough of each other! They are filling that God-given desire for intimacy!

I have watched that young love, a pure love, and I am so thrilled for them. At that age, I never knew pure love. I can tell you, I never remember being pure in my whole life. And you will know what I'm talking about if you were the victim of childhood abuse. I just never knew the word "pure" —no way. I didn't know what the word "virgin" meant. I didn't know anything of that. But I have watched this pure love between my daughter and her fiancé and it is the sweetest thing.

That desire for intimacy is a lifelong desire. And that desire was put in us by God. That desire is what some of you need to know. In this life we get just a taste of intimacy and we want it so badly, but ultimately we can't keep it.

Beloved, our desire for intimacy is fulfilled in Him! It is fulfilled in Him! He is the romance you can't get enough of. He is the constant mystery. We have been confused by measuring Him with a standard of humanity. We think He's like everybody else and we're going to just settle in to a nice comfortable relationship with Him.

Perhaps you feel you have settled into a relationship with the God of all creation. I have to tell you, we don't settle into this one when we understand that the wonders of His person are incalculable, impossible to fulfill.

We can never get enough. This is no man. He is no regular person.

I want you to go to the furthest reaches of your intellect and I want you to try to measure excellence with me. I want you to think of the things around you that speak grandeur to you. I want you to think of the wonders of creation. I want you to think of the universal order, which is so magnificent, the natural laws.

They're nothing but the mere works of His hands! Nothing but the merest suggestion of His person! And we have cheapened our walk by going for what He can do for us alone, when the real joy is growing in the knowledge of the wonders of His person!

When my husband Keith and I were in South Africa we wanted to see some giraffes. God was so sweet to show off for me.

We have cheapened our walk by going for what He can do for us alone, when the real joy is growing in the knowledge of the wonders of His person!

It's something I am always asking Him to do. I think nothing of saying, "Show off for me! I tell you what, Lord, if You'll show me, if You'll delight me, I promise You I will jump up and down." I truly believe that the more you applaud God, the more He comes in for an encore!

Anyway, as we were out driving through a field we saw one giraffe. And so I applauded God, I said, "Oh, yes! You are so good! You are so good!" Just then He brought out fifteen more! We were awed by what we saw. Keith and I just sat there and looked at the wonder of God's creativity. Ever think of those little spots on a giraffe? They are amazing.

I want to know the mind that thought that up. That is the mind of our God. Oh the wonders of His person!

And then to watch them drink—all the way down like doing the splits. I want to know the mind that thought that up. That is the mind of our God. Oh the wonders of His person!

Now I want you to think to the furthest reaches of the excellence of man. I want you to think artwork for a moment. When is the last time you just stood in front of a work of art and said, "Who did that? Who could do that?" Have you ever seen Michelangelo's work? I mean, who in heaven's name could do that?

I want you to think of the most excellent performance. Somebody just truly gifted. I want you to think of the most excellent musical score. Think for a second; just let Handel's Messiah play in your head for a second.

All of these are the merest suggestions, the tiniest fragments of what Christ has in full. He is the kind of person we will sit across from someday and say, "Tell me something else. Tell me something else. Tell me something else. Tell me something else. Tell me something else. And what do You think when You see that? And how does that make You feel? What are You thinking right now? What were You thinking when You made that? What was on Your mind?"

We will ask questions to the furthest

reaches of our imagination.

Do you remember John Nash, the one who was the subject of the film, *A Beautiful Mind*? He battled schizophrenia throughout his life, yet won the Noble Peace Prize because he was such a gifted mathematician. Now think, what is it that makes a mind able to think like that? In formulas and equations…sheer brilliance! Do you understand that is the merest suggestion of the wonders of God's person? That Christ Jesus just spoke it, and it was! Not a beautiful mind…*the* beautiful mind.

It is so sad, but we're just not getting it. I say this as the first of offenders and not with condemnation. But we just don't get the true wonder of His person. We just decide enough's enough, and start cruising on the knowledge that we have. We start cruising on that last tank and do not pursue knowing the wonders of His person.

That I may intimately and progressively know the wonders of His person.

You know, as I've watched my girls fall in love with such a pure love, I've thought so much about the Lord Jesus. I have thought, "You know, there's no going back and doing that again. I can't go back and fall in love like that. It's already done. And I didn't do it the way you were supposed to do it."

But I do get to do that one more time. No matter how old I feel—and see all the wrinkles. Women, you know what I am talking about! I look in the mirror and I think to myself, "Who are you?" Amen? And I ask God, "What have you done with my neck?"

That Christ Jesus just spoke it, and it was!

Not too long ago a good friend of mine called me and said, "Okay, Beth, I've read everything I can about menopause, and let me just say, there's no good news here." I have found that to be absolutely true! But you know what I love about the Lord Jesus? I feel totally young and beautiful with Him. I do. And so should you!

In Him our youth is renewed, the Scripture says. So see, I get to enjoy that early romance, and so do you. We get to know the intimacy our hearts yearn for because we can know Him, the eternal lover of our souls. That is the wonder of His person!

Chapter Four

Perceiving, recognizing, and understanding the wonders of His person

I want us to look at these three words: perceiving, recognizing and understanding.

First, I want you to think about perceiving. We really don't come close to perceiving God as He truly is. And one of the things we want to ask God to do with us is to help us grow in our ability to perceive Him, our ability to discern Him.

We need God's help because I believe our primary cause of errant perception is our attempt to perceive God with our injured soul-man as opposed to our undisturbed, untouched spirit-man.

Hang with me here! Let me explain what I mean.

You are made of three parts and so am I. We are made of a physical body, we are made of a soul, and we are made of a spirit. Now our soul is everything that gives us our emotions, our personality, all the things that make us—us—without the Lord Jesus. The spirit in us is our capacity to know God and to relate to God. Every single one of us is born with a spirit; it's what sets us apart from the animals. Now when we receive Christ as our savior, His Spirit takes up residency in our spirit.

You must come to that place where you realize that you really are something to God.

But here's what happens. As we seek to understand God, we are constantly perceiving Him according to our injured soul-man. Our soul has been injured by sin. And it continues to be injured by life. Injured by hurts, injured by betrayals, injured by failure, injured by feelings. If we try and perceive God through the lens of any of these things that have damaged our soul, then we end up with a warped perception of God.

For instance, let's say we try to perceive God by what we feel. Now feelings are wonderful, don't misunderstand me, but here's what happens when we perceive according to how we feel. We feel loved today, but we don't feel love tomorrow. Guess how we then view the love of God? We question whether it will be there tomorrow. And our perception of God then flows out of a very injured soul, instead of out of the Spirit.

Let's take sin—now here's something I've got to talk about. Believe me, I have been there. It is always amazing to me how we damage ourselves because of sin. And we have to understand that we will never be able to fulfill our purpose if we do not turn from our practices of sin. We will never perceive God as He truly is because sin quenches the Spirit. And when we quench the Spirit, we cannot hear Him and we cannot perceive Him.

This is so essential because everything God wants to reveal to us is through His Spirit.

That means you and I have to learn what it means to be filled with His Spirit. I Corinthians 2:9 says God wants to do more in our lives than our ears have heard, more than our eyes have seen and more than our minds have ever conceived. But it is revealed to us through the Spirit, the Scripture says.

Sin is so corrupting. Sin can ruin our lives and keep us from what God has for us.

You and I have got to learn what it means to be filled with His Spirit.

I Corinthians 5:6 is so instructive. Paul uses the yeast and the dough to show us the impact of sin. It says, *Your boasting is not good. Don't you know that a little yeast works through the whole batch of dough?*

This verse is talking about having an area of sin in our lives that is our pet area. Do you understand what I'm talking about? It's the cherished sin we have in our life. It's this yeast in the whole batch of dough. But God tells us, in verses 7-8.

> *Get rid of the old yeast that you may be a new batch without yeast...* (this is my favorite part) *...as you really are. For Christ, our Passover lamb, has been sacrificed. Therefore let us keep the Festival, not with the old yeast, the yeast of malice and wickedness, but with bread without yeast, the bread of sincerity and truth.*

Now look at the phrase, "...as you really are." I love that phrase because God wants us to understand that when we're wigged out in sin we are not acting like the person we really are. We might keep trying to say, "Lord, this is just how I am." But He says, "No, you're not. That is not how you are. You are acting contrary to who you are. You are a victor. You are more than an overcomer. I've given

you victory over that area of sin. You really
are pure."

You must come to that place where you
realize you really are something to God. And

**You must
come to
that place
where you
realize
that you
really are
something
to God.**

when you practice on-
going sin in your life, you
are quenching the glory of
God which He so desires to
reveal to you.

Perception. Perceiving
with the spirit-man.

*Lord, let Your Word
divide between soul and spirit, bone and
marrow, that we would know the difference
between what our injured soul-man is trying
to tell us and what the Holy Spirit of the living
God desires us to understand.*

Now, there is something very important I
need you to understand. Please track with me
here. My physical body has been disturbed.
I've been the victim of abuse. Not only that,
but I have done goodness knows what else
with my body. And my soul has certainly

been disturbed, because the physical abuse I have suffered has deeply touched my soul.

But you know what? Nobody has touched my spirit. My spirit is untouched, virginal, chaste, one hundred percent without yeast. No one has victimized my spirit and I have never been able to defile that. Beloved, you have something and someone within you that is totally untouched and totally undefiled! Hallelujah!

When we live the Spirit-filled life, God's Spirit comes and takes command and authority over our lives. But only when we're living out of the spirit-man instead of our injured soul-man. The more you live out of that spirit-man the more your soul-man cannot control!

Perception. Recognition. That I may perceive, that I may recognize the wonders of His person.

When I think of perceiving and recognizing the wonders of His person, I can't help but think of Isaiah 6:3. This verse tells us the angels cry to one another, *"Holy, holy, holy is the Lord God Almighty."* But it says something very important in the next phrase: *"The whole earth is full of His glory."* Why is the whole earth full of His glory? Look at Isaiah 45.

Isaiah 45:18 says, *For this is what the Lord says—He who created the heavens, He is God; He who fashioned and made the earth, He founded it; He did not create it to be empty, but formed it to be inhabited —He says: "I am the Lord, and there is no other. I have not spoken in secret, from somewhere in a land of darkness; I have not said to Jacob's descendants, 'Seek Me in vain.' I, the Lord, speak the truth; I declare what is right."*

God created all the heavens and all its vast array, and He created this tiny little thing, this speck of a speck in the universe. He is God; He took His hand and fashioned and made the earth.

But why did He create "the heavens… and the earth?" Why this one planet? What set the earth apart? Do you ever think about how wild this is, how weird this is? That we live on this small speck of a planet tucked in the middle of a vast universe, and as far as we know we are the only people on a planet? How bizarre! Why?

He fashioned and formed the earth to be inhabited by mankind so He could reveal His glory to man. His glory is His revelation to man. He picked out earth to reveal His glory because we're on it. Oh, my goodness! He created earth to be inhabited, put people on it, and then filled the whole earth with His glory so as we sought him, we would find Him.

He fashioned and formed the earth to be inhabited by mankind so He could reveal His glory to man.

We stay tucked in our offices, drive in and curse the traffic, get overwhelmed by the rush of life and never look up to behold the sunset before us and shout to God, "What glory! What glory we behold!"

Glory is constantly bursting around us and we're missing it! We're missing the wonders of His person! Every morning, and every day, and every night He is revealing Himself to us. He is revealing the wonders of His person.

God gave me these words not long ago in my quiet time as a powerful reminder of how God's glory is all around us and what a glory it is!

The whole earth is full of His glory,
extolling her maker, telling His story.

Lightning declaring, thundering praise,
the "I am here" of the Ancient of Days.

Universal order claiming,
pointing, whispering, shouting, naming,

God alone has said, then done,
and all creation came from One.

The whole earth is full of His glory,
extolling her maker, telling His story.

*The heavens declaring, the earth
groaning praise,
the evidence of the Ancient of Days.*

*Ever happening ever 'round us,
glory seeking 'til it found us.*

*Lift your eyes, behold Him now,
your King is there just behind the clouds.*

God is constantly revealing His glory throughout the whole earth, just so we'll look and see Him. He's showing off just so we'll look and see the wonders of His person.

God is constantly revealing His glory throughout the whole earth, just so we'll look and see Him.

Now look at our three words again: "That I may progressively *perceive, recognize* and *understand.*" God desires us to not just perceive and recognize the wonders of His person, but to *understand.*

Do you know what understanding is? You know those fragments of knowledge we were talking about? It is the ability to pull those fragments of information and knowledge we learn about Christ Jesus our Lord together, and as we look at them, begin

There is nothing we can't face when we know the One in whom we believe.

to comprehend them with some accuracy. Begin to accurately see who our God is.

These little fragments of knowledge are of critical importance because we live a life inundated by what we don't know. How often we say, "I have no idea…." And the only thing that will ever get us through the list of "I have no idea" is that which we do know.

II Timothy 1:12 is so dear to me. *That is why I am suffering as I am. Yet I am not ashamed, because I know whom I have believed.…*

This truth is so foundational—so

important for us to understand. This truth will get us through the toughest of times.

There is nothing we can't face when we know the One in whom we believe. Because let me tell you something, there will always be a whole lot of things we don't know, a whole lot of things we don't understand. His ways are higher than our ways. But we can know Him. We can know who He is when we don't have a clue what He's doing.

Paul was really suffering when he wrote II Timothy 1:12 —My paraphrase... knowing what he suffered...would be something like this: *I may not completely comprehend everything I'm going through, but this is why I'm not ashamed. I know Him. I know Him. That's why I wouldn't dare turn back at this point, because I know whom I've believed and I'm persuaded that He is able to guard, to keep that which I've entrusted unto Him against that day.*

Here's the picture I want you to see. The word "guard" (in some versions it is "keep") tells you why you can release your concerns to Him...why you can get settled on making your life's purpose knowing Him and why you can give everything else to Him.

This word in the Greek language is "phylasso" and it is the word from which the Greek word phylactarian is taken, which is the word —stay with me here —phylactery. A phylactery is a little box an Orthodox Jew puts on his head. It has some leather straps to hold the little box on his forehead and in the box are some little tiny papers with the Law written on them. It is their way of fulfilling God's command in Deuteronomy 6 when He told them to write the Law on their doorposts, write it on the frames of their houses, and even put it on their forehead. God's point was to have it all around them, but they took this very literally.

We can know who He is when we don't have a clue what He's doing.

And so there are pieces, statements

of God's Word, in that little box, and it is on their head. Do not forget that Paul was a Hebrew of Hebrews, a Pharisee. He was a Rabbi. He was a true teacher.

When he uses that terminology, here is what he means, "All I have to know is whom I believe in. I gotta know Christ, and everything else I can commit to His care, because my concerns are strapped to His head."

He is talking Rabbi talk here. He is saying, "My concerns are strapped on His head." That's why you can relieve them to Him. Because they're on His head. God is not going to forget your concerns. God knows what worries you. God knows what scares you nearly to death. God knows what's on your mind...let it be on His.

Must it be on both of yours? He is wearing it right at the front of His forehead. Paul said, "My concerns are written on pieces of paper, and they are bound to the head of my Savior. He will never forget, therefore I

can release and trust because I know the one
I believe in."

As I bring this to an end, I want to pray
for you. I want to pray that God will take the
truth of what you have just read and help you
apply it to your life. And one way to do that
is to write your concerns on pieces of paper.
Put them out before Him. Maybe find a little
box that you can put them in and picture when
you place those before Him that they are
going on a box strapped to his forehead.

*Father God, I pray that you have sown
an abiding Word in us. I pray we will know
we have purpose on this planet, and that
no matter what the situation may be, it will
present an opportunity that we may know
Christ and the power of His resurrection.
You know our concerns; you know our needs.
Keep them on your forehead that we might
release them from ours. That we might be
anxious for nothing, and instead choose joy.
You are it. And I give you praise. Seal the
work that you've done through this booklet, in
the mighty name of Jesus, Amen.*

— Beth Moore